GUERRILLA MARKETING
DURING TOUGH TIMES

IS YOUR BUSINESS
SLOWING DOWN?
FIND OUT WHY HERE!

JAY CONRAD LEVINSON
BEST SELLING AUTHOR WITH OVER 14 MILLION BOOKS SOLD

GUERRILLA MARKETING DURING TOUGH TIMES

By Jay Conrad Levinson

ISBN: 1-933596-10-4   Paperback

ISBN: 1-933596-11-2   e-Book

ISBN: 1-933596-12-0   Audio

Published by:

MORGAN · JAMES
PUBLISHING FOR THE REST OF US...

Morgan James Publishing, LLC
1225 Franklin Ave Ste 325
Garden City, NY 11530-1693
Toll Free 800-485-4943
www.MorganJamesPublishing.com

Cover and Inside Design by:
Heather Kirk
www.GraphicsByHeather.com
Heather@GraphicsByHeather.com

Habitat
for Humanity®
Peninsula
Building Partner

"Your guerrilla marketing talk was definitely the highlight of our seminar schedule. In fact, many veteran attendees proclaimed you as the best speaker we have presented in our eight-year history."

~ David Scroggy, Director, Comic Book Expo

"A source of inspiration for many independent entrepreneurs."

~ Booklist

"Every book by Jay Levinson is worth reading."

~ Jane Applegate, author of Succeeding in Small Business

"Slam dunk! Without exception, every person who attended our guerrilla marketing seminar said it was well worth their time. Some even commented that they were glad others did not show up because now they have a jump on their competition."

~ Julie Lopresti, Advertising Manager, Pacific Bell

"Ask almost any successful entrepreneur what the best book is for building a small business, and one of Levinson's titles will surely come up."

~ Entrepreneur Business Success Guide

"You gave us concise, practical ideas to implement directly, and virtually all of them were applicable and affordable. Our franchisers are now

committed guerrillas and they will need what is really marketing weapon number one, a book full of more of your terrific ideas. You are, by far, the best and more popular speaker we have ever had and PostalAnnex+ is sure to benefit from your presentation for years to come."

~ David Wilkey, Director of Marketing, PostalAnnex+

"After 'Guerrilla Marketing' became a best-seller, the series took on a life of its own....irrevocably tied in with the unconventional, non-textbook, and practical wisdom of guerrilla business practices for small business."

~ Home Office Computing

"A veritable plum pudding of marketing techniques and secrets."

~ Los Angeles Times

"'Wow!' is the first word that comes to mind when I think of your presentation at Entrepreneur's Day. You really gave our attendees some great advice and tactics to market their businesses more effectively and aggressively."

~ Melissa Anderson, Manager, Public Relations;
The Enterprise Corporation of Pittsburgh

"We can fully appreciate the value of your condensation of marketing techniques into a simple to use format."

~ Jerald N. Cohn, PakMail Centers of America

"Jay did a super job here in Denver. The Guerrilla Marketing Weapons Workshop was a great success, as was his talk at lunch. I heard from many of the attendees that the event was well worth the time and money spent."

~ Joyce Schlose, Manager, The Small Business Profit Center, Greater Denver Chamber of Commerce

"Dear Jay — the recent Business Solutions Forum was a huge success. Key to its success was the high quality of the keynote presentations — these presentations set the bar very high and created the right environment for the AT&T case studies that followed. In fact, one of the keynote presentations remains the subject of a great deal of conversation today. I guess it was simply delivered better and had more real content. It was yours....we thank you!"

~ Macy Jones, Director of Development, Strategic Marketing, Inc.

"Thank you for being part of INTEC's Annual Marketing Meeting last week. Your presentation was outstanding. We heard nothing but positive comments from our members."

~ Dennis C. Hardy, President, INTEC & Company, Inc.

"Thank you for the presentation 'Guerrilla Marketing for Your Small and Growing Business.' Our audience enjoyed it very much. Your contribution to the Quality Learning Series is greatly appreciated."

~ Lisa M. Finley, Marketing Coordinator, U.S. Chamber of Commerce

"Your keynote presentation was terrific. The NBIA Board, staff and audience very much enjoyed your presentation."

~ Dinah Adkins, Executive Director,
National Business Incubation Association

"Your speech at Entrepreneur's Day was great! What a good way to kick-off this conference with such a strong emphasis on marketing. Guerrilla Marketing is just what these entrepreneurs need to understand. Your style and delivery was excellent and I heard many young entrepreneurs talk about the impact it made."

~ John R. Thorne, Chairman, Carnegie Mellon

"We had well over 140 people attend the event and every single one I spoke with was pleased at the value they received and were excited about applying the concepts that you presented to them. You may be interested to know that our chamber will soon be designating its own 'guerrilla marketer' to help promote our services and programs.

~ Ben Buehler-Garcia, Group Vice President,
Tucson Metropolitan Chamber of Commerce

"We have received a great deal of positive feedback and by all standards the Conference was an overwhelming hit — the best one yet! We congratulate you on your outstanding performance that contributed to the Conference's success."

~ Lisa Schaertl and Scott Rothchild,
The Annual Catalog Conference and Exhibition

"Your comments set the stage for a healthy debate about the difficult challenges of achieving future success in an industry historically supported by tremendous asset growth and strong capital markets."

~ Gregory T. Rogers, President, FutureWatch

"The pens and pencils were definitely flying during your presentation of 100 guerrilla marketing tips. Over 85% of survey respondents gave your presentation high ratings. The others, I am sure, simply had a hard time keeping up with your rapid-fire tips, tactics and suggestions."

~ William Annesley, Chief Marketing Officer,
Invisible Fence Company

"The seminar was a huge success. I have received nothing but positive comments about his presentation. We had a great time."

~ Gary Nicholds, Williamson Medical Center

"Your presentation was absolutely fantastic and the feedback has been quite positive."

~ Karlene Johnson, Managing Director, Johnson Communications

The content was great, and I believe that most of our members either heard new material or were given the opportunity to reexamine forgotten concepts. On the whole, I would rate your presentation highly."

~ Eric J. Newman, President, North Bay
Association for Mortgage Brokers

"Your presence certainly helped to make the day a success. Your discussion of guerrilla marketing weapons and methods was pertinent to the issues facing today's business people. Our exit survey results reflected the praise I heard from many of the attendees. The audience reaction to your speech was excellent and many commented on how refreshing it was to receive not only philosophy on how to run a business, but the tools and methods they can implement immediately to see results."

~ Suzanne Clements, Retail Products Manager, The Wichita Eagle

"Marketing whiz wows area CEOs. Jay Levinson, customer analyst and author of widely published books on 'guerrilla marketing,' won over 70 Atlanta-area chief executives Tuesday. He told them how to win over customers."

~ Susan Harte, The Atlanta Journal

"Jay, thank you for your continued contribution to small biz. You are a joy to work with and I couldn't imagine the site without you."

~ Kathleen Doll, Microsoft Small Biz Website Manager

"Jay, as one who has, if not made a living, at least made some money, out of writing, I have the greatest admiration for you, not just for who and what you are, but how cogently you have been able to put your great marketing ideas into such excellently received books."

~ Gerardo Joffe, Author and successful entrepreneur

WE BEGIN WITH A BIO OF JAY CONRAD LEVINSON

Jay Conrad Levinson is the author of the best-selling marketing series in history, *"Guerrilla Marketing,"* plus 27 other business books. His guerrilla concepts have influenced marketing so much that today his books appear in 41 languages and are required reading in many MBA programs worldwide.

Jay taught guerrilla marketing for ten years at the extension division of the University of California in Berkeley. And he was a practitioner of it in the United States — as Senior Vice-President at J. Walter Thompson, and in Europe, as Creative Director and Board Member at Leo Burnett Advertising.

He has written a monthly column for *Entrepreneur Magazine*, articles for *Inc. Magazine*, and writes online columns published monthly on the Microsoft Website — in addition to occasional columns in the *San Francisco Examiner*. He also writes online columns regularly for Onvia.com, FreeAgent.com and MarketMakers.com, and InfoUsa.com in addition to occasional columns for Guru.com.

Jay is the Chairman of Guerrilla Marketing International, a marketing partner of Adobe and Apple. He has served on the Microsoft Small Business Council and the 3Com Small Business Advisory Board.

His *Guerrilla Marketing* is a series of books, audio tapes, video-tapes, an award-winning CD-ROM, a newsletter, a consulting organization, an Internet website, and a way for you to spend less, get more, and achieve substantial profits.

TABLE OF CONTENTS

2

CHAPTER 1

Tough Times Don't Have To Be As Tough As You Think

TOUGH TIMES DON'T HAVE TO BE AS TOUGH AS YOU THINK

In every down economy, some businesses lose money while others seemingly coin money. This course is designed to put you into the latter category. The plain fact is that guerrillas have an advantage during tough times. They are able to work in relatively shorter time frames. Their penchant for information enables them to market more quickly and creatively to market needs.

The guerrilla lives by different rules during tough times than during boom times. The guerrilla attacks when the competition retreats and the attack is concentrated where the guerrilla offers specific product or service advantages. Retreating companies leave voids in the market, ideal niches for guerrilla companies.

Guerrillas do not commit all their resources to any one front because they try to maintain resources for new options and for potential confrontations with the competition. Flexibility is an asset. Successful guerrilla companies try to be inconspicuous about their success, reducing the chances of being copied when attacked by their competitors.

They know many companies have scrubbed or reduced their marketing budgets to combat tough times and that it will cost those firms three dollars for every dollar formerly spent to reach the same level of consumer recognition and share of mind they previously enjoyed.

Guerrillas are aware that their prospects are more likely to recall marketing messages delivered consistently during a fragile economy, even if they are smaller and less frequently delivered. So they maintain the attitude of a guerrilla even when the economic situation is in its darkest days.

"In a dog-eat-dog economy, the Doberman is boss," said Edward Abbey, the author and naturalist. In this regard, the Doberman and the guerrilla have a lot in common.

Guerrillas know that they must seek profits from their <u>current customers</u>. They worship at the shrine of customer follow-up. They are world-class experts at getting their customers to expand the size of their purchase. Because the cost of selling to a brand-new customer is <u>six times higher</u> than selling to an existing customer, guerrilla marketers turn their gaze from strangers to friends.

This reduces the cost of marketing while reinforcing the customer relationship. To guerrillas, follow-up means marketing to some of the most cherished citizens of planet Earth — their customers.

When your customers are confronted with their daily blizzard of junk mail and unwanted email, your mailing piece won't be scrapped with the others, and your email won't be instantly deleted. After all, these folks know you. They identify with you.

They trust you. They know you stay in touch with them for a reason. So they'll be delighted to purchase — or at least check out — that new product or service they didn't know you offered. They'll always be inclined to buy from a company they've patronized instead of experimenting with a company that has not yet won a share of their mind.

When you follow up with intensity, it proves that you really care and that you'll be there when the customer truly needs you. If you haven't started a customer-stroking program yet, start it tomorrow. And whatever you do, put it in writing and determine two things: who will take the responsibility for each follow-up activity, and when that activity will take place.

In any rugged economy, the telephone is a remarkably effective follow-up weapon for guerrillas. You certainly don't have to use the phone to follow up all of your mailings to customers, but research proves that it <u>always</u> will boost your sales and profits. Sure, telephone follow-up is a tough task. But it works. Anyhow, no one ever said that guerrilla marketing is a piece of cake.

Email ranks up there with the telephone, possibly even outranks it. It's inexpensive. It's fast. It lets you prove you care. It helps strengthen your relationship. And in your subject line, you can mention the recession if your offering is in any way related to it.

Lean upon your website as well. Instead of telling your whole story with other marketing, use that other marketing to direct people to your site. Then, use the site to give a lot of information and advance the sale to consummation.

Guerrillas are able to think of additional products and services that can establish new sources of profits to them. In any kind of economy, they are on the alert for strategic alliances — fusion marketing efforts with others. This kind of cooperative marketing makes sense at all times, but makes the most sense during tough times, when companies must market aggressively while reducing their marketing investment.

Guerrilla companies cease most broadcasting and increase their narrowcasting — to customers and carefully targeted prospect lists. A faltering economy is tough. Still, when the going gets tough, guerrillas make sizeable bank deposits. Many see beauty in economic ugliness.

In gloomy economic days, when everything else seems to be shrinking, think in terms of expanding your offerings. Do absolutely everything you can to motivate customers to expand the size of their purchase. Prove that buying right now is a sagacious move because of the tough times.

In marketing to customers and to non-customers, show that you are fully aware of the economic situation and that you have priced your goods and services accordingly. Even though your marketing is always truthful, exert even more of an effort during bad times to make it sound truthful. Candid language is a powerful weapon. Admit that times are tough; admit that people must be extra careful when buying things; explain that you're fully aware of the economy and taken special steps because of it.

This course will help you investigate a treasure-trove of marketing tactics that can help you weather the toughest of times. But learning about them is only half the battle. It's when you begin putting them into practice — you'll assure that the real tough times are those faced by your competition.

GUERRILLA EXERCISE:

Ask yourself ten easy questions:

1. Am I attacking or retreating on the marketing front?

2. Am I marketing with more than one marketing weapon?

3. Is my marketing exposed to my target market consistently?

4. Are some of my marketing funds directed at current customers?

5. Am I making use of the telephone in my marketing?

6. Do I take advantage of marketing with email?

7. Is my website working to advance my marketing thrust?

8. Do I have any strategic alliances with other companies?

9. Do I automatically try to enlarge the size of each transaction?

10. Does my marketing admit that times are tough?

THE MORE YOU ANSWERED "YES" TO THESE QUESTIONS, THE MORE PRIMED YOU ARE TO MARKET IN TOUGH TIMES.

GUERRILLA ACTION STEPS:

1. Spend one hour examining the websites of your competition. Compare them with your own site and determine three ways you can improve your site.

2. Study today's newspaper to see what kinds of tactics other types of companies are using to combat a down economy. Put into writing at least three of these tactics.

3. Make a list of the marketing efforts you are using specifically to combat the economic slowdown. The longer your list, the better.

CHAPTER 2

The Importance of Stressing Value

THE IMPORTANCE OF STRESSING VALUE

Whatever you do, don't make the mistake of thinking that the right price for tough times is the lowest price. Price becomes secondary during hard times; people are searching for value. If you offer customers great values — in the form of more durable products, more encompassing services, or long-term economy, you'll earn higher profits than if you target your marketing solely to skinflints.

Tough times require superb values. And that's what guerrillas offer. If you're truly a guerrilla, you'll also eliminate any perceived risk of buying from you by stressing your money-back guarantee, your liberal warranty and your deep commitment to service. Mention the names of others who have purchased from you.

A word about guarantees: the longer yours is, the more profits you'll earn. Offer a one-month guarantee, and some people will return your offering and ask for a refund. Offer a six-month guarantee and fewer people will make returns, thinking there is no rush to do it. Offer a one-year guarantee, and the number of returns drops even more.

Now, wrap your mind around offering a lifetime guarantee. If you do, more people will purchase from you, figuring that a lifetime is a very long time, but because of zero pressure to return what they've bought, hardly any will return it.

The net result to you: more sales and fewer returns. Meaning: the longer the guarantee, the more profits you'll earn.

Do you sell a high-priced product or service? It seems that a high price will be detrimental to you during challenging times. But just the opposite is true. If you offer high-priced items, use those tough times as a selling tool. Explain to people that during a rugged economy, it is crucial not to waste money. Therefore, they should protect their money by spending it wisely and not making a mistake. Mistakes can be financial disasters during a down economy. Makes sense, doesn't it?

Still, in any economic situation, every guerrilla knows that the number one factor influencing purchase decisions is confidence. And the road to confidence is paved with credibility.

Having the lowest price won't help you much if your prospect doesn't trust you in the first place. Offering the widest selection and the most convenience won't aid your cause if your prospect thinks you're a crook.

You've got to face up to the glaring reality that prospects won't call your toll-free number, access your website, mail your coupon, come into your store, visit your trade show booth, talk to your sales rep, talk to you on the phone, or even accept your generous freebie if they aren't confident in your company.

Time zips on by. Your prospects can't afford to waste it or their money with companies that haven't earned their confidence. In order to earn that confidence — no stroll in the park, as you've most likely learned — you've got to use specific guerrilla marketing weapons and use them properly. I emphasize "properly" because even a smart bomb isn't a valuable weapon if it lands on your foot.

Guerrillas think in terms of getting down to the business of achieving and deserving credibility. All their marketing materials, whatever they say or show with their main message, also carry a "meta-message" — an unstated, yet powerful communiqué to prospects.

The meta-message for Deuce Cleaners of a superbly written direct mail letter on very inexpensive stationery is going to be quite different from the meta-message of the same letter for Ace Cleaners on costly stationery that looks and feels exquisite.

The paper stock carries a strong meta-message. So does the real or metered stamp. The typeface speaks volumes and the printed — or handwritten — signature is even more eloquent. The Ace Cleaners letter has superb stock, a clear and elegant typeface and a hand-signed signature, using blue ink and a fountain pen. These are tiny details. Tiny but nuclear-powered. Why? Credibility is why.

Not surprisingly, the Deuce Cleaners letter, even though worded exactly like the Ace Cleaners letter, will not draw as healthy a response because of its weak meta-message. <u>A powerful meta-message inspires confidence.</u>

Entire marketing plans fall by the wayside because inattention to seemingly unimportant details undermines the prospect's confidence — even if that confidence was earned elsewhere.

An amateurish logo or meme makes your company seem like an amateur. Any hint of amateurism in your marketing indicates to your prospects the potential for amateurism elsewhere in your company — throughout your company.

Does this mean that cheap stationery, a plain Jane website, fuzzy type, and poor English destroy your credibility? Not entirely. But shabbiness in these areas certainly does not contribute to your credibility.

<u>Absolutely everything you do that is called marketing influences your credibility</u>. The influence will be positive or negative, depending upon your taste, intelligence, sensitivity, and awareness of this power.

Be aware of it the moment you start operating your business, and if not then, right now. Begin the quest with the name of your company, your logo, your theme line, location, stationery, business card, package, brochure, business forms, interior decor, website, fusion marketing partners, even the attire worn by you and your people.

Communicate even more credibility with the building you're in, the people you employ, the technology you use, the follow-up in which you engage, the attention you pay to customers, the testimonials you display, your trade show booth, your signs, and surely the neatness of your premises.

The way your phones are answered can gain or lose credibility for you. Just yesterday, I decided not to make an expensive purchase from a store I had called, simply because they put me on telephone hold for too long. Minor detail? Maybe, but somebody else now has my deposit check.

You gain credibility with your advertisements, listings in directories, columns and articles you write, and the talks you give. You gain it with your newsletter. You gain even more by your support of a noble cause such as the environment. All these little things add up to something called <u>your reputation</u>.

The most important word in marketing — <u>commitment</u> — is something that also fuels your credibility. When people see that you are maintaining consistency in your marketing, especially during tough times, they'll assume you're just as committed to quality and service — and can deliver on them regardless of the economy.

All of your weapons must communicate the same meta-message — one that fits in with everything else in your marketing and with the reality of your offerings. You don't need a Lincoln Continental identity to succeed with a bait shop.

Credibility is not automatic but it is do-able. Give a seminar. Work hard for a community organization. Nudge customers into referring your business. Word-of-mouth is omnipotent in the credibility quest. The idea is for you to establish your expertise, your authority, your integrity, your conscientiousness, your professionalism, and therefore — your credibility.

When that PR person gets you into the newspaper, make reprints of the article and frame them, include them on your website, into your brochure, pop them into your newsletter, put them on your counter, stick them in your store window. Cost? A bit of time. Result? A lot of credibility.

Trade shows can enhance your credibility and so can free demonstrations. Free consultations can do wonders for it and so can free samples. Do glitz and glamour enhance your credibility? They do —- but be careful that you don't send out the wrong message. If you're a discounter, glitz can sabotage your identity.

Want a shortcut to credibility? Run a full-page ad in a regional edition of a national magazine. Just running the ad won't net much credibility for you, but the reprints you display, mail, incorporate into other marketing, and proudly disseminate will. They'll all proclaim "As advertised in Time magazine." And if they don't say, Time, they'll say some other prestigious publication.

All the credibility that millions of readers attach to the magazine — they suddenly attach to you. I'm not talking zillions of dollars here. I'm talking of a few thousand — and just one time. It's a small price to pay for credibility. You can get details about incredibly low costs for incredibly credible magazines by getting the free media kit from Media Networks, Inc. at 1-800-225-3457.

During a shaky economy, people are attracted to solid businesses. You can prove your stability by consistently stating your message and by remembering that credibility equates with profitability.

GUERRILLA EXERCISE:

1. Are all of your marketing messages emphasizing value?

2. Do you offer a long guarantee?

3. Can you use your price, high or low, as a selling tool?

4. Have you taken concrete steps to enhance your credibility?

5. Are you aware of the meta-message conveyed by your marketing?

ONCE AGAIN, EACH "YES" ANSWER POSITIONS YOUR COMPANY TO THRIVE DURING TOUGH TIMES.

GUERRILLA ACTION STEPS:

1. List five things you are doing now to earn extra consumer confidence and credibility.

2. List five additional things you can and will do to earn even more confidence and credibility.

3. Put into writing exactly why your offerings provide exceptional value.

CHAPTER 3

Using Consent Marketing Now More Than Ever

USING CONSENT
MARKETING NOW
MORE THAN EVER

Seth Godin, who has co-authored three books with me, authored "Permission Marketing: Turning Strangers into Friends and Friends into Customers," and in doing so, changed my entire outlook about marketing and can dramatically change the beauty of your bottom line.

Seth, once a student of mine, now has enlightened me to the presence of two kinds of marketing in the world today. The first, most common, most expensive, most ineffective and most old-fashioned, is <u>interruption marketing</u>. That's when marketing such as a TV commercial, radio spot, magazine or newspaper ad, tele-marketing call, or direct mail letter interrupts whatever you're doing to state its message. Most people pay very little attention to it, now more than ever because there is so much of it and because many minds now unconsciously filter it out.

The opposite of interruption marketing is the newest, least expensive, and most effective kind. It's called <u>permission marketing</u> — because prospects give their permission for you to market to them.

It works like this. You offer your prospects an enticement to volunteer to pay attention to your marketing. The enticement may be a prize for playing a game. It could be information prospects consider to be valuable. It might be a discount coupon. Perhaps it's membership to a privileged group such as a frequent buyer club, a birthday club. Maybe it's entry into a sweepstakes. And it might even take the form of an actual free gift. All you ask in return is permission to market to these people. Nothing else.

Alas, you'll have to use interruption marketing in order to secure that important consent. And you'll have to track your costs like crazy, figuring how much it costs you to gain each permission — easily figured by analyzing your media costs divided by number of permissions granted.

Once you've embarked upon a consent marketing campaign, you can spend less time marketing to strangers and more time marketing to friends. You can move your marketing from beyond mere reach and frequency and into the realm of trust.

Once you've obtained consent from your prospects, your marketing will take on three exciting characteristics. It will be anticipated, meaning people will actually look forward to hearing from you. It will be personal, meaning the messages are directly related to the prospect. And it will be relevant, meaning you know for sure that the marketing is about something in which the prospect is interested.

Consent marketing is not about share of market, not even about share of mind. Instead, it's about share of wallet. You find as many new actual customers as you can, then extract the maximum value from each customer. You convert the largest number of prospects into customers, using your invaluable consent to accomplish this. You focus your marketing only on prospects and not on the world at large.

Let's use an existing coed summer camp as an example of permission marketing in action. The camp uses interruption marketing to run ads at camp fairs and in magazines that feature other ads from summer camps. But the ads do not attempt to sell the summer camp. Instead, they focus solely upon motivating prospects to send for a video and a brochure, upon securing their consent to accept your marketing with an open mind.

Once the prospects receive the video, they soon see that it, too, does not try to sell the camp. It is geared only to get consent to set up a meeting. But having seen a video of the camp facilities, activities, happy campers and attentive staff, the prospect is all set to say yes to a personal meeting.

At the in-person meeting, the sale is closed. And once a camper attends the camp for one summer, chances are pretty darned good he or she will not only stay for several more summers, but also will bring along a brother, a sister, a cousin, a schoolmate or a friend —- or all of these.

Notice that the only goal of each step is to expand permission for you to take another step rather than making the ultimate sale. Who uses consent marketing these days? Record clubs. Book clubs. Marketers who offer a free brochure. Even my own website at GMarketing.com offers you something free, just for signing up with us — in affect, gaining permission to market to all those who sign up.

The biggest boon to consent marketing is the internet — but only by those who treat it as an interactive medium and not like TV. As clutter becomes worse, consent becomes more valuable. The moral: since only a limited number of companies within a market niche can secure consent, get moving on your own consent marketing program pronto.

In addition to your consent marketing program, you've also got to realize that all customers are not created equal. Your "A" list customers spend more, buy more frequently, refer your business to others, happily complete customer questionnaires, give you names for your referral list, and are pleasant people overall.

Your "B" list customers buy from you, but aren't necessarily bright spots on your customer list. Your job as a guerrilla is to treat both of these groups of customers very well. You must treat those "B" list customers like royalty — because that's what they expect and that's what they deserve.

You should treat your "A" list customers like family — because they are more profitable to your company and they help you maintain your sanity. A few months ago, my wife and I ate at a restaurant we've frequently visited. When presented with our check, we were given a ten percent discount along with a VIP card that would give us ten percent off on all future meals. The waitress said, "You're very valued customers to us and this card is to show our appreciation."

Have we eaten there many times since? Have we recommended the restaurant to our friends? You know that the answers are a resounding "yes," and you can just imagine how we feel about that restaurant. But it doesn't take a discount to show your gratitude to your best customers. Just treating them extra-special and acknowledging that you appreciate their business is usually enough. Still, they do deserve special treatment.

During tough times, it doesn't cost you one extra cent to render extra superlative service, but you can be sure that your customers notice it. Your "A" list customers should receive advance notices of sales, of new products or services that you offer, of information that can help them succeed at their own goals.

Just think of the attention and kindness that you give to your friends. They appreciate you for it and happily return your friendship. Then think of the extra attention you probably lavish upon members of your own family. It's usually more than you give to your friends — not a whole lot more, but enough so that they feel like family. So it should be with your "A" list and "B" list customers.

Life is not always simple black and white. There are also many gray areas. If you're not certain whether a customer should be on your "A" list or "B" list, it's best to err on the side of caution and treat those in the gray area as though they are members of your family.

GUERRILLA EXERCISE:

Go over your customer list and try to identify your "A" list and "B" list customers. This will take a bit of your time, but it will be worth that time investment.

Consider actually "firing" some of your customers — those who take up the most time, have the most problems, and do not prove their loyalty to you. Firing a customer is never fun, but it is worth your time — especially during a down economy.

GUERRILLA ACTION STEPS:

Put into writing a list of the things you do to treat your "B" list customers like royalty.

Put into writing a list of the things you do to treat your "A" list customers like family.

Formalize a program where your "A" list customers realize that you actually do give them special treatment.

CHAPTER 4
Free And Almost Free Marketing

FREE AND ALMOST FREE MARKETING

Some kinds of marketing are very expensive. Other kinds are relatively inexpensive. This lesson is about marketing that is free or nearly free. Of the many kinds of free marketing, such as publicity or word-of-mouth, we'll concentrate here upon two types of free or nearly-free marketing:

1. Enlarging the size of each transaction — free

2. Going after repeat sales — nearly free

The first, enlarging the size of each transaction, costs you absolutely nothing. The customer has already decided to make a purchase from you. All you've got to do is make it a larger purchase. You can do that by offering a deluxe version, by offering the item or service as part of a package, or by turning the single purchase into some kind of subscription. That means if a person hires you to wash their carpets, you say, "I can give you a very special price if you sign up for carpet washing every three months."

The cost to enlarge the transaction is zilch. Customers don't become offended when you make the offer. Instead, many of them appreciate it. A bookseller decided to put three books, all related, into a wicker gift basket. If a person was interested in one of them, the bookseller would point out the gift basket. Very often, the person would buy the whole package, tripling the size of the transaction. The cost of marketing the package was zero.

You can be certain that car dealers, such as Mercedes-Benz, provide a lot of upgrade training to their sales staffs. A person drives to a Mercedes showroom with the idea of buying the least expensive model. But that's probably not going to happen — due to that upgrade training. Upgrading the size of a transaction is simple because the person has already decided to buy from you.

You job now is to come up with deluxe versions and package offers. Perhaps you can even link up with one of your fusion marketing partners — and make a "commission" on each sale for which you're responsible. Again, that represents no cost to you.

Repeat sales are a method of nearly free marketing — one with a payoff very disproportionate to your investment. Why do you suppose most businesses lose customers? Poor service? Nope. Poor quality? Nope. Well, then why? Apathy after the sale. Most businesses lose customers by ignoring them to death. A numbing 68% of all business lost in America is lost due to apathy after the sale.

Misguided business owners think that marketing is over once they've made the sale. WRONG, WRONG, WRONG. Marketing begins once you've made the sale. It's of momentous importance to you and your company that you understand this. I'm sure you will by the time you've come to the end of this lesson.

First of all, understand how guerrillas view follow up. They make it part of their DNA because they know it now costs six times more to sell something to a new customer than to an existing customer. When a guerrilla makes a sale, the customer receives a follow-up thank-you note within 48 hours. When's the last time a business sent you a thank-you note within 48 hours? Maybe once? Maybe never? Probably never.

The guerrilla sends another note or perhaps makes a phone call 30 days after the sale. This contact is to see if everything is going all right with the purchase and if the customer has any questions. It is also to help solidify the relationship. The what? The relationship. Guerrillas know that the way to develop relationships, the key to survival in an increasingly entrepreneurial society, is through assiduous customer follow-up and prospect follow-up. And we haven't even talked yet about prospect follow-up.

Back to the customer. Guerrillas send their customers another note within 90 days, this time informing them of a new and related product or service. Possibly it's a new offering that the guerrilla business now provides. And maybe it's a product or service offered by one of the guerrilla's fusion marketing partners.

Guerrillas are very big on forging marketing alliances with businesses throughout the community — and using the Internet, throughout the world. These tie-ins enable them to increase their marketing exposure while reducing their marketing costs, a noble goal.

After six months, the customer hears from the guerrilla again, this time with the preview announcement of an upcoming sale. Nine months after the sale, the guerrilla sends a note asking the customer for the names of three people who might benefit from being included on the guerrilla's mailing list. A simple form and postpaid envelope is provided. Because the guerrilla has been keeping in touch with the customer — and because only three names are requested — the customer often supplies the names.

After one year, the customer receives an anniversary card celebrating the one-year anniversary of the first sale. Perhaps a coupon for a discount is snuggled in the envelope.

Fifteen months after the sale, the customer receives a questionnaire, filled with questions designed to give the guerrilla insights into the customer. The questionnaire has a paragraph at the start that says, "We know your time is valuable, but the reason we're asking so many questions is because the more we know about you, the better service we can be to you." This makes sense. The customer completes and mails the questionnaire.

Perhaps after eighteen months, the customer receives an announcement of still more new products and services that tie in with the original purchase. And the beat goes on. The customer, rather than being a one-time buyer, becomes a repeat buyer, becomes the kind of person who refers others to the guerrilla's business. A bond is formed. The bond intensifies with time and follow-up.

Let me put this on numeric terms to burn it into your mind. Suppose you are not a guerrilla and do not understand follow-up. Let's say you earn a $200 profit every time you make a sale. Okay, a customer walks in, makes a purchase, pays, and leaves. You pocket $200 in profits and that one customer was worth $200 to you. Hey, $200 isn't all bad. But let's say you were a guerrilla.

That means you send the customer the thank-you note, the one-month note, the three-month note, the six-month note, the nine-month note, the anniversary card, the questionnaire, the constant alerting of new offerings. The customer, instead of making one purchase during the course of a year, makes three purchases. That same customer refers your business to four other people. Your bond is not merely for the length of the transaction but for as long as say, twenty years.

Because of your follow-up, that one customer is worth $400,000 to you. So that's your choice: $200 with no follow-up or $400,000 with follow-up. And the cost of follow-up is not high because you already have the name of the person.

The cost of prospect follow-up is also not high and for the same reason as with customers. Prospect follow-up is different from customer follow-up. For one thing, you can't send a thank-you note — yet. But you can consistently follow up, never giving up and realizing that if you're second in line, you'll get the business when the business that's first in line messes up. And they will foul up. You know how? Of course you do. They'll fail to follow up enough.

GUERRILLA EXERCISE:

1. Make a list of three ways you can enlarge the size of each transaction.

   A. _____

   B. _____

   C. _____

2. Make a list of five ways you can follow up with each customer.

   A. _____

   B. _____

   C. _____

   D. _____

   E. _____

3. Make a list of three ways you can follow up with each prospect.

   A. _____

   B. _____

   C. _____

GUERRILLA ACTION STEPS:

1. Keep track for one month of the follow-up mail, post-cards, telephone contacts and email follow ups that you receive from businesses that you patronize. Ask yourself which follow-ups motivate a purchase on your part.

2. Think back about the purchases that you've made during the past year. Determine which ones were the result of the business enlarging the size of the transaction. Then, figure which of those methods that you might utilize.

CHAPTER 5

Mining Your Customer List For Fun And Profit

MINING YOUR CUSTOMER LIST FOR FUN AND PROFIT

Your best source of new customers during tough times is your list of old customers. It's as though you live next to a bountiful gold mine, owned entirely by you — but you never take a single nugget, and you consistently bemoan your lack of profits.

A sad scene, yet one that is repeated daily in every nation on planet Earth. This shouldn't happen to you — but the chances are that it does, and this lesson is devoted to stopping it.

The bountiful gold mine is your customer list. On that roster of wonderful people are the names of customers who know other wonderful people, poised and ready to get onto your customer list themselves. All they need is a gentle nudge. And who do you think is the chief nudger?

You are — if you're a guerrilla. If you're canny enough to know that the richest source of new customers is old customers, then you're ready to mine that list for names that will be forthcoming — and on a yearly basis at that — if you simply ask for them. Is it that easy? You betcha.

The man who led the nation in insurance policy sales a few years ago was interviewed, focusing upon his astounding success — because he sold twice as many policies as the agent who finished in second place.

He explained that as soon as his client would sign on the dotted line, this agent would reach into his attaché case and withdraw a large memo pad. In the presence of his new client, he would write numbers on a blank page: 1, 2, 3, 4 and 5. Then, he'd ask his client for the names of five people who might benefit from a policy such as the client just purchased. The client, feeling positively, almost always furnished the names. Five isn't an unreasonably high number, plus it's nice and specific.

Guerrillas learn a lesson from this example. So they put into writing, a guerrilla referral program. How do you get such a program to work? Four steps:

1. At the time of the initial purchase, ask for the names of five people who might benefit from the product or service your customer just purchased.

2. In six months, send a brief letter reminding that you know the importance of customers, then asking for the names of three people who could benefit by doing business with you. Provide a postpaid return envelope.

3. A year after that, ask for the names of four people who could gain by becoming your customers. Perhaps this time you'll send a little gift, whether or not the customer furnishes names.

4. Once a year, for as long as you're in business, ask your customers for the names of three, four or five people who

might gain by becoming your customers. Because of your guerrilla follow-up, expect a healthy response.

When it's appropriate, ask if you can use the name of the customer when contacting the prospect he or she recommended. Talk about door-openers! Thank the customer for taking the time to provide these valuable names. This guerrilla referral program is simply common sense, yet how can you explain the absence of such programs at most American businesses? Think there might be a connection between high business failure rates and few referral programs?

Guerrillas know that it now costs six times more to make a sale to a prospect than to an existing customer, so they do everything in their power to increase the size of their customer list, then market with guerrilla gusto to customers and acquaintances of customers. Just realize that along with the repeat business of customers, can come a gold mine of names of future customers. Be sure you stake a claim to your fair share of nuggets.

The cost of an active referral program is tiny compared with the potential for profits such a program can mean. The best way to get the names of new customers from old customers? <u>Simply ask for them.</u>

As a guerrilla, you've been staying in touch, so your customers want you to succeed and will happily comply with your request for, say, three names. Ask for them, provide a postpaid envelope, and you'll soon see this tactic is pure gold. There are other ways to tap into your enormous referral power:

Identify potential references. List everyone with whom you have worked in the past three years, and others who know you well.

1. <u>Note on your list what you would like a reference to do.</u> There is more than one kind of reference: use of their name, calls for you, and written testimonials. Be specific. Think especially of what you would like past customers to say. You'll be surprised at how willing they are to say it.

2. <u>Ask pleasantly</u>. Asking politely generates good references. Everybody understands the need for a business reference. It's a reasonable thing to ask for. If properly asked, most people will applaud good work.

3. <u>Request name use.</u> First, phone and ask the potential references if you can use their names — either in talking with a potential customer or on your company brochure. Allow them the chance to say no.

4. <u>Get telephone references.</u> You can tell by people's voice tones if their references will be good. If references agree to your using their names, ask if they will take phone inquiries. Create a stable of references who will speak highly of you when called.

4. <u>Obtain a letter.</u> If the telephone reference is better than average, ask for it in writing. Tell the reference that a few short words will do, such as, "Ms. Atwood's service was outstanding. We intend to use her on 90% of our future jobs."

Why don't people give more referrals? Because they're afraid you'll foul up and they'll be blamed. Guerrillas continue to develop <u>new customers all the time</u> because know they're losing old customers all the time:

- 1% of customers die.

- 3% move away.

- 5% develop other business relationships.

- 9% leave for competitive reasons.

- 14% are dissatisfied with the product or service

- 68% leave due to an indifference on the part of an employee.

The way around these irrevocable statistics? With a referral program that is active, alive, constantly used and part of the way you run your business.

GUERRILLA EXERCISE:

1. Look at your customer list and realize deep in your heart that it's your most precious business asset. Used properly, it can lead to untold profits...and with a minimal investment on your part.

2. Create a referral program in writing. It should call for you to contact these customers on a regular basis — not merely for follow-up marketing, but with the purpose of getting names of potential future customers. This is especially easy with email.

GUERRILLA ACTION STEPS:

1. Actually write the letter you will send to customers, the letter that asks for the names of people who might benefit from doing business with you.

2. Select five customers you will call by phone to secure the names of people who are potential customers. Call them and tell them that you'd appreciate these names as a way of holding down your marketing costs. By seeing how simple it is to get names, you'll be motivated to call more customers — or ask one of your employees to do it for you. Hint: It helps the most if you are the one who makes the call.

CHAPTER 6

Community Involvement During Tough Times

COMMUNITY INVOLVEMENT DURING TOUGH TIMES

Guerrillas know well that people want to do business with friends instead of strangers if at all possible. You must have their insight that you dive into an ocean of friends with community involvement. You become involved with the community by helping it. It becomes involved with you by helping you. Marketers need friends. From these friends come business associates, marketing partners, investors, employees, customers, prospects, suppliers and referrals.

Becoming involved with the community means more than joining clubs. It means contributing your brains and energy to the community. It means working hard to make your community a better place. You get to prove your conscientiousness and noble efforts with the work you do instead of the words you say.

One of the keys to marketing — keeping it very personal, because the more personal the marketing the better — is in establishing relationships through networking. And one of the richest sources of networking opportunities is the community. You serve on committees. You go to little league games. You help set up parades, holiday decorating programs, Thanksgiving Day turkey races, Fourth of July celebrations. People see you in action. They see that you're a person of action, a person who keeps their word. So when you say something in a marketing context, they tend to believe you. When you make an offer, they know it's not going to be bogus. You've proved yourself in the community.

There are wrong ways to demonstrate community involvement as well. If you volunteer to work on a committee but are never available for meetings, or if you sponsor a little league team and don't show up for games, you're proving yourself to be crass and superficial, probably sucking up the community to get business instead of working for it for altruistic reasons. Consumers are more sophisticated than ever these days. People know the difference between serving the community and serving yourself. If you're not willing to devote honest time and energy to your community, you're better off skipping this weapon and leaving it to the real guerrillas in your community. I just hope for your sake that none are your direct competitors.

Your community is not merely defined by geography. Guerrillas become involved with their industrial community, though it may reach from coast to coast, or across the ocean. Digital communities are springing up all over the place as the world goes online. Whatever the size or scope of your community, the Guerrilla Rule remains the same: do unto others as they hope you will do unto them. As part of the community, they are hoping for your help, not your hype.

While you're involved with your community, be sure that you're attuned to their problems. Listen for the "ouch". Guerrillas know that it's easier to sell the solution to a problem than to sell a positive benefit. That's why they position themselves as problem-solvers.

A well-known axiom of marketing has always been that it is much simpler to sell the solution to a problem than it is to sell a positive benefit. For this reason, guerrillas position their companies to be ace problem-solvers... especially during tough times.

They hone in on the problems confronting their prospects, then offer their products or services as solutions to the problems. Almost all individuals and companies are beset with problems of one sort or another. Your job, as a right-thinking guerrilla, is to spot those problems. One of the ways to do this is through networking in your community.

Networking is not a time to toot your own trombone, but to ask questions, listen carefully to the answers, and keep your marketing radar attuned to the presence of problems. After learning them, you can contact the prospect and talk about the prospect's problems and your solutions to those nasty dilemmas.

You can also learn of problems that require solving at trade shows, professional association meetings, prospect questionnaires, and even sales calls.

As you already know, people do not buy shampoo; they buy clean, great-looking hair. That means selling a benefit. A way that some shampoos have achieved profits is by reassuring people that the shampoo cleans hair, then stressing that it solves the problem of unmanageable hair — a benefit and a solution to a problem.

Right now, products and services that are enjoying success are those that help people quit smoking, lose weight, earn more money, improve health, grow hair, eliminate wrinkles, and save time. These are problem-solving products and services.

You can be sure that some of these can also be positioned as offerings that accentuate a positive. But savvy company presidents saw to it that their offerings were positioned as things that could eliminate a negative. Your biggest job is to be sure your products and services do the same.

Perhaps you'll have to undergo a major repositioning. That's not bad if it improves your profits. Far more doors will be open to you if you can achieve it.

Maybe you know right off what the major problems facing your prospects are. Your marketing should highlight these problems. Then, it should offer your product or service as the ideal solution. If you don't know the problems, knock yourself out learning them. Regardless of the benefits you offer, realize that their importance is generally overshadowed by the problems confronting a prospect.

It's really not that difficult to position your offering as a problem-solver. But once you do, you'll find that the task of marketing and selling become a whole lot easier in a hurry. You'll have to examine your offerings in the light of how they affect your prospects. So what if they are state-of-the-art? That pales in comparison with their ability to reduce your prospect's overhead. So what if they are lower in price than they used to be? That's nothing compared with their ability to help your prospects combat loneliness.

Those prospects care about saving money, to be sure. But they care far more about feeling alone and unloved. If you can solve that problem for your prospects, buying what you sell will be very easy for them.

Prospects don't really care about your company; they care about their problems. If you can solve them, then prospects will care a great deal about your company, and they'll want to buy what you are selling.

Guerrillas lean upon case histories to prove their problem-solving acumen. They make certain to include in their marketing plan both the problem and the solution — to guide those who create marketing materials from wandering off in the wrong direction.

Sales training in guerrilla companies involves a discussion of problems, problem-spotting, problem-discussing, and problem-solving. Sales reps learn the nature of prospect problems from one another. Sharing their insights helps the entire company.

Amazingly, even though this all makes sense, many companies are unaware of the importance of problem-solving. They're so wrapped up in the glories of their product or service that they are oblivious to how well it solves problems. So they sell features and neglect benefits. They sell the obtaining of positives instead of the eliminating of negatives.

Keep the concept of problem-solving alive in your mind, your marketing materials, your sales presentations, and your company mission. Be sure your employees are tuned into the same wave length. Once this happens, I have a feeling that you're going to be one happy guerrilla.

GUERRILLA EXERCISE:

1. Make a list of the community organizations where you live — or online communities where you can become involved. Then, list the things you can do for the community. Don't offer to do anything that you can't accomplish with excellence. So be selective.

2. Make a phone call, send a letter, or send an email volunteering your services. Take the time to actually do it after you've completed this lesson. He who hesitates is not a guerrilla.

GUERRILLA ACTION STEPS:

1. Make a list of the problems that your business can solve. The longer your list, the more profits you'll earn during an economic downturn.

2. Examine all of your marketing efforts, online and offline; to be sure you address your problem-solving skills. Make the necessary changes to ensure that you're putting those skills in front of your audience. Don't neglect the positive benefits you offer, but highlight your ability to solve problems.

CHAPTER 7

Attracting New Business During Tough Times

ATTRACTING NEW BUSINESS DURING TOUGH TIMES

When the going gets tough, the tough get new business. Many of your competitors have pulled in their horns and cut back on their marketing. This means new opportunities for you to get new customers. The obtaining of precious new business is a whole lot easier than you may have imagined — but only if you have the mindset of the guerrilla.

One of the least understood secrets of successful marketing is the ease with which new business may be won. As powerful as you may be with that knowledge, your power increases when you comprehend the importance of gaining that new business in the first place.

You already know that it costs you six times more to sell something to a new customer than to an existing customer — which is why guerrillas market so caringly and consistently to their customers — there is a constant need to increase your customer base. Therefore, you've got to be willing to turn cartwheels in order to get a human being converted into a real live paying customer. Break even or even lose money in the quest for a new customer because your investment in securing these precious souls will be returned manyfold.

Once your prospects become customers, they're a source of profits for life — because guerrillas like you know the crucial importance of non-stop follow-up. The follow-up increases your profits while decreasing your cost or marketing.

But let's get back to those non-customers and consider a potent guerrilla tactic to win their business and transfer them from the twilight zone to your customer list, where they belong. The tactic begins with a phrase. A powerful guerrilla phrase to emblazon amidst your memory cells is "pilot project."

It is often difficult to get a company or a person to agree to do business with you, especially in a shaky economy. It is much simpler to get them to agree to a mere pilot project. Even if companies or individuals are unhappy with their current suppliers, they may be reluctant to sever the relationship and sign up with you — just in case you turn out to be flaky.

But you defuse that reluctance when you assure them that you don't want to get married — and get all their business. You only want to become engaged —- and get a simple pilot project. That's certainly not asking for much.

Pilot projects are very tempting to companies and to individuals because they allow these good people to see if you're as good as you say you are, without going too far out on a limb. Even if the project is a bust, it was only a pilot project. No big deal.

But if the project is a success — well then, that certainly indicates that a larger project should be undertaken, then a larger one still, and eventually, all the business. Moral? It's tough to get an okay for all the new business. But it is far less tough to get an okay for a pilot project.

The concept of aiming for pilot projects may be applied as easily to a service business as a product business. If you perform services, offer to perform them for only part of the customer's needs, not all of them. Offer to perform them for a test period only, something like six weeks or so — maybe even less if you feel that less time will be enough for you to prove your worth and value.

If you sell products, request that during the pilot project, they be given prominent display, proper signage, and ample shelf space. But because it's only a pilot project, ask for this only for a limited time, or with a limited order. Will your products generate profits? This simple pilot project will tell.

Guerrillas are wary of wooing new business by offering discounts — because they know darned well that customers who purchase by price alone are the worst possible kind, disloyal, expensive to maintain, and in the end, only one-ninth as profitable as loyal customers who stick around because of value or service, quality or selection. But these self-same guerrillas are very willing even to lose money on customers — for the first sale only — if the customers focus on things other than mere cost.

Pilot projects are rarely profit producers all by themselves. But they open the door to a world where profits abound, a world where relationships are lasting. That's why savvy companies and individuals say "yes" to offers of pilot projects. These projects are inexpensive learning and high potential earning opportunities. Hey! Why not do a pilot project on pilot projects?

I am very aware that during a spiraling economy, you've got to make a dynamite proposal — even to get the go sign for a pilot project. I'm also aware that many businesses fall on their faces when they make a proposal. Having secured an appointment to make a proposal, guerrillas stand out and shine.

They know that it's at proposal time that the rubber meets the road. To get the best ride possible, you've got to present a guerrilla proposal. This lesson will show you how to create one.

There are poor proposals, which rarely get the business for you. There are good proposals, which might get the business for you. And then, there are guerrilla proposals, which usually get the business for you. If you present anything but a guerrilla proposal, it means that all the marketing you've done up till that time has probably been wasted. Sheer agony.

The companies that get the business realize that all the time and energy they've put into wooing a prospective customer has been mere groundwork for the dazzling display of business acumen that will be made apparent when they get down to the business of making an actual proposal.

Guerrillas follow these ten steps to make sure that their courtship activities lead to a long-term business marriage — destined to flourish and prosper.

1. Guerrillas are always positive that they have qualified their prospects so that the marriage doesn't die during the honeymoon. Getting your prospect's attention is only a tiny part of assuring a lasting relationship. When your prospect shakes hands with you and says "Let's do it!" — You've got to be certain that both of you will gain. You must be right for them and they must be right for you. Chemistry counts in both people-to-people marriages and in business-to-business pairings.

2. Guerrillas start immediately to warm up the relationship by building rapport with their prospects. They never want to walk into a prospect's office or conference room as a complete stranger. That's why they see their job as forging a bond before making the proposal. They know well that it's much easier to do business with friends than strangers.

3. Guerrillas identify a real need that their prospects have and know in their hearts that they can fill that need better than anyone else. They keep foremost in their minds the truism that people give their business to firms that can help them solve their problems and exploit their opportunities.

4. Guerrillas make absolutely certain that the prospect to whom they are making their proposal can use their products or services right now, and not at some future date down the road. They present their proposals only to people who are the ultimate decision-makers and can give them the go-ahead immedi-

ately without having to check with higher authorities. During an economic slowdown, this is of paramount importance.

5. Guerrillas rehearse their presentation till they've got it down pat. They decide ahead of time exactly what they want to show and tell, then plan intelligently, back their chosen words with graphics, and always ask for the order at the conclusion of the proposal. Non-guerrillas may make a decent proposal, but usually fail to ask outright for what they want

6. Guerrillas prepare a document to leave with their prospects right after the proposal has been presented. The document summarizes the high points of the proposal, is completely self-contained, and includes important facts and figures that might have bogged down the actual presentation.

7. Guerrillas design their proposals in a way that addresses their prospect's goals clearly and unmistakably. They are able to do this with a single sentence that proves they are directed and oriented to those goals. They find ways to repeat that sentence several times during the presentation of their proposal — up front, in the middle, at the end, and in the written document they give to their prospect when the presentation is completed.

8. Guerrillas present their proposals in a logical manner so that one point flows naturally to the next, making the proposal very simple to follow. They know that the organization of

their proposal is nearly as important as the content. Their proposals prove beyond doubt that they are qualified to get the business, and then that they are particularly qualified and deserving of the business right now.

9. Guerrillas speak and write in the first person, aligning everything they say with the prospect's business. They make it a point to talk about the prospect's business and not about their own. In fact, they only speak of their own business in terms of how it can help the prospect's business. This requires homework and guerrillas always do their homework before presenting any proposal.

10. Guerrillas are quick to use the services of a talented art director or a PowerPoint presentation to help them reinforce their points visually, knowing that points made to the eye are 68% more effective than the same points made to the ear. They always try to visualize what they are saying, and they realize that if the visuals are shoddy or look home-made, they are sabotaging themselves.

When you are making a proposal, you must make the prospect like you, like your company, and love what your company can do for them. You must then actually ask for the business at the conclusion of the presentation. Never underestimate the brute power of straightforwardness.

Because guerrillas are ultra-keen about follow-up, they follow-up their proposals with a thank-you note within 24 hours of the presentation. That follow-up also includes a phone call to be sure no questions are left unanswered, to see if there is anything else the prospect would like to know, and to establish a start date for doing business together. The follow-up should be directed to the person who has the authority to say "yes."

The more data you have about your prospect, the better your proposal will be and the more likely it is to land the business for you. The better you prove that you understand the prospect's competitive situation, the more likely that prospect will want your help. And the better the chemistry is between your people and the prospect's people, the more likely it is that you'll get exactly what you want.

Never fail to keep in mind the power of a personal bond. And never forget that when you're making a proposal, your three greatest allies are your knowledge of the prospect, your enthusiasm during the presentation, and the personal bonding you have already established.

GUERRILLA EXERCISE:

1. Make a list of prospects who have not yet been converted to customers. Then, select the ten who will most likely be most profitable for your business. Pull out all the stops when contacting these ten and learn what works for you and what doesn't. After you've completed your high-potency marketing to those ten, take on the rest of your prospect list, using what you learned during the original ten.

2. Create a proposal for the single best prospect of all. Then knock yourself out making an appointment to make the proposal. You may earn the business and you'll definitely learn more about your ability to create winning proposals.

GUERRILLA ACTION STEPS:

1. Put into writing the specifics of a pilot project you can perform for a client. The more specifics you have, the easier it will be to sell that project.

2. Practice making your proposal to a current customer. Ask that customer for feedback and suggestions. This will not only deepen your relationship with that customer, but will also help you hone your presenting skills and the quality of your proposal.

CHAPTER 8

The Importance Of Service During Tough Times

THE IMPORTANCE OF SERVICE DURING TOUGH TIMES

If ever there was a time to emphasize your impeccable service, it's when the economy is heading south. Sure, all business owners care about their customers, but guerrilla marketers prove they care.

It's very easy to care about your customers, even easier to say that you care. But unless you take steps to show them that you care, they might be wooed away by a competitor. Your marketing can say all the right words and tell customers how important they are to you. But you've got to prove your dedication to customers — and prospects — by taking concrete steps beyond mere words.

Guerrillas know that there's a world of difference between customer care and customer attention. Many companies lavish attention upon their customers, but only the guerrillas excel at caring and know how to make customers feel sincerely cared for. Here are twenty ways that they do it:

1. Prepare a written document outlining the principles of your customer service. This should come from the president, but everyone should know what it says and be ready to live up to it.

2. Establish support systems that give clear instructions for gaining and maintaining service superiority. They help you out-

service any competitor by giving more to customers and solving problems before they arise.

3. Develop a precise measurement of superb customer service and reward employees who practice it consistently. Many will, if you hire people who really want to render great service, and don't just do it because they should.

4. Be certain that your passion for customer service runs rampant throughout your company and not just at the top. Everyone should feel it.

5. Do all that you must to instill in employees who meet your customers, a truly deep appreciation of the value of customer service. They should see how this service relates to your profits and to their future.

6. Be genuinely committed to providing more customer service excellence than anyone else in your industry. This commitment must be so powerful that every one of your customers can sense it.

7. Be sure that everyone in your company who deals with customers pays very close attention to the customer. Each customer should feel unique and special after they've contacted you or been contacted by you.

8. Ask questions of your customers. Then listen carefully to their answers. Ask customers to expand upon their answers.

9. Stay in touch with your customers. Do it with letters, email, postcards, newsletters, phone calls, questionnaires and, if you can, at trade shows.

10. Nurture a human bond as well as a business bond with customers and prospects. Do favors for them. Educate them. Help them. Give gifts. Play favorites. Take them out to the ballgame or the opera. Your customers deserve to be treated this special.

11. Recognize that your customers have needs and expectations. You've got to meet their needs and exceed their expectations. Always? Always.

12. Understand why successful corporations such as 3M define service as "conformance to customer requirements." This means that true guerrilla service is just what the customer wants it to be. Not easy, but necessary.

13. Keep alert for trends, and then respond to them. McDonald's operates under the axiom, "We lead the industry by following our customers."

14. Share information with people on the front line. Disney workers meet regularly to talk about improving their service. Information-sharing is easier than ever with new communications technologies. Share information with customers and prospects by having a website that is loaded with helpful data. More and more, this is becoming mandatory.

15. Because customers are humans, observe birthdays and anniversaries. Constant communication should be your goal. If you find an article in the media that will help a customer, send a copy of the article to that customer. Have you ever received such an article from one of your suppliers? Probably not. That's why your attention to a customer will stand out so brightly.

16. Consider holding "mixers" so customers can get to know your people better and vice-versa. Mixers are breeding grounds for human bonds.

17. Invest in phone equipment that makes your business sound friendly, easy to do business with, easy to contact and quick to respond. Again, technology makes this easier than ever. Along with phone equipment, let customers know they can contact you by fax and e-mail.

18. Design your physical layout for efficiency, clarity of signage, lighting, handicap accessibility and simplicity. Everything should be easy to find.

19. Act on the knowledge that what customers value most are attention, dependability, promptness and competence. They just love being treated as individuals and being referred to by their name. Don't you?

20. When it comes to customer service, Nordstrom is a superstar, though Disney gives them a run for their money, and so do

the Ritz-Carlton Hotels. The Nordstrom service manual is eloquent in its simplicity: "Use your good judgment in all situations. There will be no additional rules."

Guerrillas send postage-paid questionnaire cards and letters asking for suggestions. They fix the trouble areas revealed and know well the relationship between proving their care and success

GUERRILLA EXERCISE:

1. Put into writing a list of the ways you offer remarkable good service. The longer your list, the easier it will be for you to thrive during a rugged economy. Augment that list by adding three items of service that you have not stressed before. When all else is equal, the company that offers the best and the most services is the one that will win the customer. Now, post that list on your website.

2. List the technologies you now employ to render superlative service: a fax machine, voice-mail, an autoresponder, a toll-free number, a cell phone, a pager — so that you make customer contact as simple as possible. To learn of a new service that makes it simpler than ever, visit www.500PLUS they let you have a toll-free 500 number along with a matching website and email address. The cost is far less than you'd imagine. Most of all, be sure you have a content-rich website that sees things from the customer's point of view.

GUERRILLA ACTION STEPS:

1. Think back upon services rendered by other companies, services that impressed you. Try to adapt those services to your own company so that you are a stand-out

when it comes to service. Nordstrom, Disney and Ritz-Carlton Hotels conduct special meetings that address nothing but service. Employee and customer suggestions are solicited. Do the same for your company. With a limited budget and a tight economy, exceptional service can make the crucial difference.

2. Think of one service that is offered by none of your competitors, a service that your customers are sure to appreciate. Then, do all in your power to market this service. By doing so, you'll be able to jump start your reputation for great service.

CHAPTER 9

Making Yourself The Talk Of The Town

MAKING YOURSELF
THE TALK OF
THE TOWN

Word-of-mouth marketing referrals come to companies automatically if they utilize a broad array of marketing weapons
over a long period of time. But guerrillas, as patient as they are, try
to shortcut the process of obtaining positive word-of-mouth.

One way they do it is with brochures printed especially for
people who are first-time purchasers. This is because of a
phenomenon called the "moment of maximum satisfaction."
That moment lasts from the moment a person makes a purchase
till 30 days past that time. During this period the person is most
likely to spread the word about his purchase, conveying his
enthusiasm and yours to all who will listen. If you hand such a
person your new customer brochure, you are putting the right
words in the right mouths at the right time. Small wonder your
word-of-mouth will pick up.

Another way to obtain healthy word-of-mouth marketing is to
ask this question: Who else do your customers patronize? Then,
do a favor for those people. Example: a restaurant opened in my
community and asked that question. The answer turned out to be:
hairstylists. So the restaurant distributed coupons good for two
free dinners to all the styling salon owners within a two-mile radius

of the restaurant. The salon owners would eat their free meals, and then talk up the restaurant in their salons, generating loads of business for the restaurant. By recognizing that the salon was the nerve-center of the community, the restaurant was able to succeed without spending one cent for advertising.

You can also become the talk of the town with public relations. Public-relations means exactly what it says. But it is also accurate to say that it means publicity-free stories and news about you and/or your company in newspapers, magazines, newsletters, and house organs, on radio and TV, and in any other type of media.

Here's what is good about publicity: It is free. It is very believable. It gives you and your company a lot of credibility and stature. It helps establish the identity of your business. It gives you authority. It is read by a large number of people. It is remembered.

Many entrepreneurs feel that there is no such thing as bad publicity; that as long as you get your name out there before the public, that's a fine thing. But guerrillas know that bad publicity leads to bad word-of-mouth marketing, known to spread faster than wildfire. Bad publicity is bad. Good publicity is great.

There are even some bad things about good publicity, though I only mean bad in a relative sense. You have no control over publicity. You have no say-so as to when it runs. You have no control over how it is presented. It is rarely repeated. You cannot buy it. You cannot ensure its accuracy.

On balance, however, publicity is an excellent weapon in any well-stocked marketing arsenal. And any marketing plan that fails to include some effort at public relations is a marketing plan that isn't going all out. And during the days of a faltering economy, it's a marketing plan bordering on stupidity.

Public-relations offers, as an unstated but ultra-valuable benefit, decades of staying power. Reprints of positive publicity can be framed, made parts of brochures, included in ads, put onto flipcharts, and leaned upon for precious credibility. The day the story appears is a heartwarming one, but the years afterward are when the marketing power abounds. When you can do it, use reprints of the story to empower your marketing. But you can't always do it.

When I was advertising my self-published book *Earning Money Without a Job* (*since* revised for the nineties and published in 1991 by Henry Holt and Company, New York) in various magazines and national newspapers, I was spending about $1000 per ad. Each ad was bringing in about $3000 in sales. The book was not available in bookstores and could be purchased only through my mail-order ad. Then a reporter from the San Francisco Chronicle purchased a copy of my book. Because I lived in the vicinity, and because he took a liking to the book, he called to see if he could come to my home and interview me, and asked if he could bring along a photographer. It didn't take me long to extend a warm welcome to him and his camera-bearing associate.

The interview lasted about an-hour and included a brief photo session. A few days later, an article about me and my book appeared in the main news section of the newspaper. Accompanying it was a photo of me. Well into the article was the address to which the $10 purchase price (now it's less) could be sent. Within a week, I received over $10,000 worth of orders! The article had not solicited orders, did not really try to sell the book, and mentioned the address and selling price in a place where only serious readers of the article would find them. More than $10,000 in sales, and the marketing didn't cost me one penny.

As wonderful as I felt about the results, I felt just as frustrated at not being able to repeat the process. I sent the article to other newspapers, letting them know I was available for interviews. I continued to advertise the book, still achieving a fair degree of success. But never again have I been able to earn so much money with so little effort. Because my mama didn't raise a moron, I have made reprints of the article and used them as parts of mailings and press kits. So I have received a bit more mileage from the publicity. Although I know of similar stories, and indeed have arranged and taken part in them, never has the value of PR hit home as sweetly as in that instance.

The reporter felt that my book was newsy, since it promised honest information on how people could earn a good living without having to hold down a job. And that is probably the single most important factor in obtaining free publicity: providing news worth publicizing.

A fascinating P.S. to that PR tale is what happened to the reporter, Mel Ziegler, who interviewed me. He took the concepts of my book to heart, quit his job at the *Chronicle*, and opened a store, the first of an empire, called Banana Republic. Before you read one more word, read these: _the media needs you more than you need them_. They need news. They hunger for news. Their unquenchable need for news is why people read them, listen to them and view them. If you have news or can make news or can create news, you are exactly what the media is looking for.

Marcia Yudkin, who knows a thing or six about publicity, gives us six steps to free publicity, based upon her book by the same name. I alert you to them here:

1. Find a news angle for your headline.

2. Present the basic facts for the angle of your headline in the first paragraph of your press release.

3. Gather or create a lively, fascinating quote that elaborates on the basic facts for the second paragraph of your release.

4. Elaborate still further on the basic facts in your third paragraph.

5. End your release with the nitty-gritty details about prices, addresses, dates, phone numbers, and registration data if any. Keep this to one paragraph.

6. Email it, send it out, or hand it to your buddies who work for the media. It helps immensely if you have a specific editor or producer who you can refer to by name.

How do you generate something newsy for the news media? Announce something new about your business or group. Write about what's unique and unusual about your business. Tell of an upcoming event. Write of the connection between your offering and what's in the news right now. Announce the results of a survey or research poll you conducted or even one you read about. Tell the community who won your essay contest. Tie in with a holiday or anniversary, especially a city event. Write of the connection between your business and a current trend. Make a controversial claim or at least, a very surprising claim. Make a humorous announcement. Put it into an eye-catching headline and you're off to the races for free publicity, appearances on talk shows — profits for a minimal investment.

Let me clarify here that if you want to, you can pay for public relations. You can hire a PR person, pay him or her a monthly fee or a project fee-anywhere from $500 to $25,000 per month- and let that person do what is necessary to secure free publicity. PR people are experts at it. They have the contacts, the experience, and the insights. They have made all the errors, they have learned from them, and they are usually well worth their fees. But because you are a guerrilla, I want to let you know in this chapter, of ways you can do what PR people do. That way, you'll be able to get the publicity and you won't have to pay anyone a dime.

Moment of truth time: The best way to succeed at public relations is to have publicity contacts-people at the media who you know on a first-name basis. It's one thing to mail a proper press kit to the proper managing editor at a publication. It's another thing to call Nancy at the paper and say, "Nancy, let's have lunch tomorrow. I have some information that will definitely interest your readers and I want you to have it first. I'll pop for the lunch."

Nancy, because she enjoys free lunches, but primarily because she knows and trusts you, has lunch with you. Never forget how hungry the news media are for news. If you have real news, they'll listen. So Nancy listens and the next day, there's a story about your product or service or company in her newspaper. When you pay a PR pro a steep fee, you're paying for a gob of Nancys, and those publicity contacts are usually well worth the price.

One of the most important public relations tools is the annual report. As a rule, entrepreneurs don't publish one. But why not? It need not conform to the usual annual report sent to shareholders. It need not talk money. It can be a report that contains information valuable to your customers. When you do publish such an annual report, send some copies to the media. Let them enjoy your creativity. Nudge them to give that creativity some "ink." And by all means, send your annual report to your prospects.

Members of the press are frequently invited to "press parties." At these parties, cocktails or beverages and a meal or hors d'oeuvres are served, and frequently a presentation is made. It's a short one, but affective and hard-selling. The purpose is to woo the press with wining and dining, and then win their hearts with a dramatic presentation of the facts. Naturally, the facts are about a new business or a new direction for an old business. It's no surprise that the press coverage following these parties is tremendous. Guerrillas hold their press parties at unique places such as ferry boats, railroad cars traveling to interesting destinations, penthouses, haunted houses, parks, baseball diamonds, zoos, and art galleries.

A major-league PR pro once told me that nearly 80 percent of the news is "planted"-sent to the media by publicity firms and lobbying groups. Sometimes planted news deals with political topics; sometimes it deals with industrial topics; and sometimes it deals with products or people. That PR pro repeated what insiders know-newspapers are hungry for real news. If you can furnish it, they'll gladly publish it. But telling a newspaper that you are having a sale is not news. Informing a radio station that you have started a business is not news. News needs a slant to it, a hook that will capture the attention of the reporter, let alone the public.

Guerrillas love the free press coverage they get from the big newspapers, but they rarely overlook the small ones. There are many of them and nearly all of them count. They never send more than one release at a time, and they are quick to learn of the myriad of PR opportunities online, discussed in *Guerrilla Marketing Online, Second Edition.* There I go again, blowing my horn and pumping up your profits.

The best marketing plans usually call for a combination of advertising and public relations and the website. Those three go hand in hand in hand. One is highly credible but gives you no control. The other has less credibility but gives you complete control. The third is one we're continuing to learn about because its opportunities are endless. Together, all three supply most of the pieces of the marketing puzzle.

When the circus comes to town and you put up a sign, that's advertising. If you put that sign on the back of the elephant and you march the elephant through town, that's sales promotion. If the elephant, with the sign still on his back, tramples through the mayor's flower garden and the paper reports it, that's publicity. If you can get the mayor to laugh about it and forgive the elephant and then ride in the circus with no hard feelings, then you truly understand guerrilla publicity.

Advertising is the most expensive method of getting out the word. Direct marketing is the next most expensive method. Being online comes in next when it comes to expense. And PR is the least expensive, but is the most time-consuming.

If you know PR, you should know what the media does not like. It's a pretty obvious list: hemming and hawing, wasted time, frivolous questions, incomplete sentences, bad writing, people who cannot take no for an answer, people who don't really believe in what they're calling or writing about, ugly persistence, demanding natures, bad listeners, people who constantly interrupt, lack of common sense, and blatant attempts to advertise under the guide of real news.

Why does well-intention PR go awry? Same reason businesses fail. Same reason marketing fails. Same reason advertising fails. It's failure to follow-up. If you're too busy to make an average of four phone calls for every media outlet you've contacted, you should turn your PR over to a pro who has the time and expertise you may lack.

If you have a yogurt shop and send out a release that says, "Best yogurt in town," you're like to be greeted by a big ho-hum. But if you sponsor a charity drive, put up a display and sign in front of your store, hand out samples of your yogurt to passers-by who read your sign, link up with a local celebrity, and then invite the media to check you out for a story, they now have a newsy and valid reason to do a story about your yogurt shop. Did I say it was easy? Never did. Did I say it helps your business? I certainly say that now.

I haven't even mentioned the plethora of public relations and sponsorship opportunities now available on the Internet. Chances abound for you to spread the good word about yourself in cyberspace by word-of-mouse, as you'll soon discover during your weekly surf. Sponsorship of many sites visited by your prospects is not costly. Just as with offline PR, most online PR is free and requires tireless research on your part. But it will be worth your effort.

There are many online sources for building your own media list. Don't rely totally on free resources for your publicity efforts. They typically are not updated frequently enough to be totally accurate or complete. A good way to collect media names which are current and actually writing for your target market is to be alert when reading trade magazines for the writers' names and contact information. Experiment with using personalized news services to receive articles about your industry, and then comb those articles for the writers' names. Get to be on a real first name basis with Google.

Just remember what the smartest of the PR pros know all too well: without publicity, a terrible thing happens — nothing.

GUERRILLA EXERCISE:

1. Make an outline for a "first-time customer" brochure. This is where you'll have the most control over your word-of-mouth marketing.

2. Make a list of other types of businesses that your customers patronize, such as styling salons or restaurants.

3. Make a list of the media in which you'd most benefit from free publicity. The list should include both online and offline media.

GUERRILLA ACTION STEPS:

1. This is tough, but tough times call for tough tactics. The tactic I recommend most highly for this lesson is for you to list three people at the media you've selected as most ideal — then get in touch with these people personally. Do it by email, telephone, but best of all — in person. The more media contacts you get, the more you'll become the talk of the town...and at no cost.

2. Come up with a list of three things about your business that are newsy. Perhaps they'll be in the area of product. Possibly they'll connect with your service. Maybe they'll be about new items or services that you offer. The three things you can dream up will be three tickets to free publicity.

CHAPTER 10

Online Marketing In A Shaky Economy

ONLINE MARKETING IN A SHAKY ECONOMY

One thing is for sure about the Internet, and that is that nothing is for sure about the Internet. The newest, biggest, most mysterious, most misunderstood and most promising marketing opportunity in history is the one offered by the advent of the internet. Every day, online marketing gets bigger, better, and more helpful both for marketers and for consumers. Still, three facts must be understood by all who would hope to become online guerrillas:

a. Online marketing will only work if you understand marketing.

b. Online marketing means a lot more than having a website.

c. Online marketing is only one percent of all marketing.

Remember that there are 100 guerrilla marketing weapons, and online marketing is only one of them. In most cases, you can't market online only with any expectation of success. Yet, the entire media world is becoming fragmented. There are regional editions of magazines, zone editions of newspapers, cable TV stations that reach local communities, local radio stations, and targeted mailing lists. Where does everything come together?

It all happens online. Slowly but certainly, people are learning that the whole story exists online — that all the details they must learn before making a purchase are ready to be studied online. The entire Internet phenomenon is part of human evolution, and humans learning how to interact in cyberspace is also part of evolution. You don't have to be reminded that evolution takes place over a long period of time. The Internet is here and everybody knows it, but not everybody is online yet, and not everybody online is ready to make purchases yet. They will. But not quite yet.

A key fact to remember is that <u>you've got to continue marketing with traditional media</u>. Your website marketing and your website needs marketing. Even when the Internet has achieved a market penetration comparable to that of the telephone, you must continue marketing using time-honored methods. TV revolutionized the marketing scene, but most of the big TV advertisers also market their offerings in places other than the tube. TV is part of their marketing mix, but not the entire potion.

When marketing with the traditional media, you're going to have to devote time and space to heralding your website because many people will want to know where they can get more information. Your website is where. No media offers you the comprehensiveness of the web. That's why you need it to flesh out your marketing. The world is learning to buy things in a new way and that way is online. But the learning process is still in process.

Pinning down the right way to do guerrilla marketing online is akin to grabbing a handful of smoke to see what it feels like. Online marketing is the essence of amorphousness and will be for a long time, constantly changing as new heroes of technology try to figure out how it can best serve the public while bestowing profits upon the companies employing it. Exciting online technologies are being unveiled so frequently they're becoming humdrum.

Of the billions of dollars being wasted by small business due to a misunderstanding of the comprehensiveness of online marketing and the reality of online consumers — a huge portion is wasted on websites. They are created and posted with obliviousness to their place in the cosmos. Guerrillas wouldn't dare waste money on their websites. They know the ground rules in cyberspace when it comes to earning consistent profits on the web. Those profits come when you equally emphasize eight elements.

The first element is planning. That means you must know ahead of time exactly what you wish to accomplish with your website.

The second element is content. That's what's going to attract visitors to your site, then keep them coming back for more visits on a regular basis.

The third element is design. There's a "hang or click" moment when people first see your site. Should they hang around or click away? Design influences their decision.

The fourth element is involvement. Guerrillas take advantage of the Net's interactivity by involving visitors rather than just requiring that they read.

The fifth element is production. This refers to putting your first four elements online. Easy-to-use software can do this job for you.

<u>The sixth element is follow-up.</u> People visit your site, email you, ask or answer some questions. Guerrillas respond to their email, stay in touch.

<u>The seventh element is promotion.</u> You must promote your site online by registering with search engines and linking with other sites, while promoting it offline in mass media, mailings, wherever your name appears.

<u>The eighth element is maintenance.</u> Unlike other marketing, a website requires constant changing, updating, freshening, renewing nurturing. Like a baby.

It was once believed that websites had to be long to be valuable, but the increased awareness of the precious nature of time is causing online marketers to rethink this concept. Websites narrowly targeted to specific groups are brief and valuable. Guerrillas know the value of being concise.

An overall website may be vast, but within it are tiny segments targeted with precision for small niches. In this way, huge guerrilla companies can have the warmth and close connection of small guerrilla start-ups.

Once you've got even the spark of a notion to go online, let that spark ignite thoughts of how you'll promote your site. Have the insight to know <u>this means thinking imaginatively about two worlds.</u>

The first is the online world, where you'll think in terms of multiple links to other sites, in terms of banners leading to your site, search engines directing browsers to your site, postings on forums alerting onliners to your site, chat conferences heralding your site, recommendations of your site by internet powers, emailing to parties demonstrably interested in learning about the topics covered on your site, writing articles for other sites in return for links back to your site, mentioning your site in your email signature, advertising online to entice people to your site, preparing an online version of your press kit to publicize your site online, and connecting with as many other online entities as possible, all in a quest to make your site part of the online community, an internet landmark to your prospects, a not-to-be-missed feature of the web.

The second world in which your imagination should run rampant in a mission to achieve top-of-the-mind awareness of your site is the offline world. Most of the population of the real world still resides there. That's where they continue to get most of their information — for now. And that's where you've got to let them know of your online site — teeming with information that can shower them with benefits — for their business or their lives or both.

Tout your site in your ads, on stationery, on your business cards, on signs, on brochures, fliers, Yellow Pages ads, advertising specialties, package, business forms, gift certificates, reprints of PR articles, in your catalog, newsletter, and classified ads. Mention it in your radio spots, on television. More than one company now has a jingle centered on their website. Never neglect to direct folks to your site in direct mail letters and postcards, in all your faxes, almost anywhere your name appears. If the world begins to think that your last name is dotcom, you're going about your offline promotional activities in the right way.

Some companies think that by including their site in tiny letters at the bottom of their ad or by flashing it at the end of their TV commercial, they're taking care of offline promotion. They're not. All they're doing is going through the motions. Talk about your website the same way you'd talk about your kid — with pride, enthusiasm and joy. Make people excited about your site because they can see your pride. Will local or industry newspapers write about your online site? Of course they will if you make it fascinating enough for their readers. That's your job. Promotion will get them to your site. Killer content will get them to make return trips.

What people want online is a question guerrillas ask themselves a lot. Whether it's for fun or work or something else, understanding a consumer's motives once he or she logs on is a necessity. But the experts don't seem to agree on what people want. Some folks see the web as a vast, new field for advertising messages, assuming that while people may want to do something else, if we can entice them with flash, we can sort of trick them into paying attention to our products and services.

Guess what? That's not gonna happen.

Other folks seem to subscribe to the notion that people online are looking for entertainment on the Internet and therefore they construct messages aimed at persuading while playing. And, in other cases, the time-honored direct-response model wins out: Grab people when you can, get 'em to take an action, and then market, market, market. The answer may be that the consumer has and wants a lot more control than we give him/her credit for.

Today, webmeisters are in control. Sort of. In a perfect cyber-world, people will be in control. Sort of.

Two recent studies shed light upon this dilemma. One was conducted by Zatso. The other was conducted by the Pew Research Center. Zatso and Pew. Those guys didn't spend much time reading "how-to-name-your-company" books, I guess. Still, both of their studies illuminated the answer as to what people want to do online.

The answer, as most answers, is very utilitarian: People want to accomplish something online. They're not aimless surfers hoping to discover a cybertreasure. Instead, the average Net user turns out to be a goal-oriented person interested in finding information and communicating with others — in doing something he or she set out to do.

Look at the Zatso study. "A View of the 21st Century News Consumer" looked at people's news reading habits on the web. It revealed that reading and getting news was the most popular online activity after email. The guerrilla thinks, "That means email is number one. How might I capitalize on that?"

One out of three respondents reported that they read news online every day, with their interests expanding geographically — local news was of the most interest, U.S. news the least.

Personalization was seen as a benefit, too. Seventy-five percent of respondents said that they wanted news on demand and nearly two out of three wanted personalized news. The subjects surveyed liked the idea that they, not some media outlet, controlled the news they saw. They feel they're better equipped to select what they want to see than a professional editor. Again, control seems to be the issue. Again, guerrillas think of ways to market by putting the prospect in control.

The Pew Research Center study revealed that regular Net users were more connected with their friends and family than those who didn't use the Internet on a regular basis.

Almost two-thirds of the 3,500 respondents said they felt that email brought them closer to family and friends — significant when combined with the fact that 91 percent of them used email on a regular basis. That's 91 percent. It took VCRs 25 years to achieve such market penetration.

What did people in this study seem to be doing online when they weren't doing email? Half were going online regularly to purchase products and services, and nearly 75 percent were going online to search for information about their hobbies or purchases they were planning to make. Sixty-four percent of respondents visited travel sites, and 62 percent visited weather-related sites. Over half did educational research, and 54 percent were hunting for data about health and medicine.

A surprising 47 percent regularly visited government web sites, and 38 percent researched job opportunities. Instant messaging was used by 45 percent of these users, and a third of them played games online. Even with all the hype in the media, only 12 percent said they traded stocks online.

What does this mean to e-marketers in tough times? It means that if you're constructing a site for goal-oriented consumers, you'd better make sure you can help facilitate their seeking. Rather than focus on entertainment, flash, and useless splash screens, the most effective sites are those that help people get the information they want when they need it. Straightforward data, information that invites comparison, and straight talk are going to win the day.

A client buddy of mine showed me his website which heralds his retail location and attempts to sell nothing online. He said it has been the biggest moneymaker in the history of his 35-year old company. Then he apologized for its lack of glitter and special effects. He asked how his site could be so successful even though it lacked anything to add razzmatazz and dipsydazzle.

Now, you know the answer.

GUERRILLA EXERCISE:

1. Write down the three questions you are asked most by your prospects and customers. The answers to those questions should be the starting point for the content on your website.

2. Answer this question: why do you want a website in the first place? The more focused your answer, the more valuable your website will be to you.

3. List what you have on your website that will involve visitors? Is it a free newsletter to which they might subscribe? A sweepstakes they may enter? A daily or weekly tip that is emailed to them regularly?

GUERRILLA ACTION STEPS:

1. Make a list of the other media you'll use to promote your online presence.

2. Review the eight steps necessary to create a winning website and ask yourself if you've paid enough attention to all eight.

Put a checkmark next to each of the eight that you've emphasized.

_____ Planning

_____ Content

_____ Design

_____ Involvement

_____ Production

_____ Follow-up

_____ Promotion

_____ Maintenance

Don't forget, you must equally emphasize all eight —
or else.

CHAPTER 11

The Freebies That Can Lead To Serious Profits

THE FREEBIES
THAT CAN LEAD TO
SERIOUS PROFITS

These days, there seem to be two kinds of businesses: givers and takers. Giver businesses are quick to give freebies to customers and prospects. The freebies may be gifts, but more likely come in the form of information. The right information is worth more than a gift and often even worth far more than money.

In fact I've added a new personality trait to my list of characteristics possessed by successful guerrillas. I've always known they were blessed with infinite patience and fertile imaginations. I've written in awe of their acute sensitivity and their admirable ego strength. I've raved about their aggressiveness in marketing and their penchant for constant learning.

Now, I'm impressed, but not surprised, at their generosity. They are, every single one of them, generous souls who seem to gain joy by giving things away, by taking their customers and prospects beyond satisfaction and into true bliss. They learn what those people want and need and then they try to give them what they want and need absolutely free.

The result? Delighted prospects who become customers and delighted customers who become repeat and referral customers. Those are huge payoffs during the days of a bear market.

What kind of things do guerrilla marketers give away for free? Let's start with a list of ten and your mind will be primed to dream up ten more:

1. They give gift certificates to their own business, whether the certificates are for products or services.

2. They give printed brochures to anybody who requests one.

3. They give electronic brochures, on audio and video, once again to people who ask for them. And they are quick to offer their free brochures in their other marketing.

4. They give money to worthy causes and let their prospects and customers know that they support a noble cause, enabling these people to support the same endeavor.

5. They give free consultations and never make them seem like sales presentations. They truly try to help their prospects.

6. They give free seminars and clinics because; they realize that if their information is worthwhile, it will attract the right kind of people to them.

7. They give free demonstrations to prove without words the efficacy of their offerings.

8. They give tours of their facilities or of work they've accomplished elsewhere, again transcending any standard marketing tools they might employ.

9. They give free samples because they know that such generosity is the equivalent of purchasing a new customer at a very low price.

10. They give invaluable information on their website, realizing that such data will bring their customers and prospects back for more, thereby intensifying their relationships.

In addition to these ten, guerrillas are highly creative in dreaming up what they might give for free. Of course, many advertising specialties such as calendars and scratch pads, mouse pads and ballpoint pens are emblazoned with their names and theme lines, but they seem to exercise extra creativity as well.

Case in point: When an apartment building went up, signs proudly proclaimed that you get "Free Auto Grooming" when you sign a lease. Soon, the occupancy rate was 100 percent. The salary they paid the guy who washed the tenants' cars once a week was easily covered by the difference between 100 percent occupancy and 71 percent occupancy, the usual occupancy rate in that neighborhood.

That means your task is clear: Think of what might attract prospects and make customers happy. Be creative. Be generous. Then, be prepared for a reputation embracing generosity, customer service, and sincere caring.

Today's customers are attracted to giver companies and repelled by taker companies. What kind of company is yours?

During an economic downturn is the time to think freely. This is the time to think as hard as you can, of what you can give away to your prospects for free. If you can possibly give away your product or service for a limited time, you have a good chance to habituate your prospects to your offering and a great chance to prove your service superiority.

The idea behind this strategy is: <u>give your prospects an ownership experience for free</u>.

If you can enable your prospects to feel like your customers, you're acting just like a guerrilla marketer. You're in business because you offer a product or service that delivers desirable benefits. You're in business because you're better than many of your competitors. You're in business because you want to earn hefty profits consistently.

As a guerrilla, you surpass customer satisfaction and allow those who patronize your business to experience customer bliss. They can tell how conscientious you are by means of your follow-up and the way you pay attention to details in their life and business. Customers of guerrillas are as contented as customers can get.

That's why you must give serious consideration to transforming all of your prospects into customers. If they won't do it by purchasing what you have to offer, regardless of your investment in marketing, perhaps they'll purchase what you have to offer if they first can try it <u>at absolutely no cost</u>.

If they have the experience of owning what you offer, they'll understand the advantages of being your customer. And then, they'll be far more likely to actually make the purchase.

This means that your prime marketing investment will be your freebie. It will be a limited time use of your product or a limited time use of your service. You'll be giving those valuable things away for free, risking that you'll get nothing in return. But if you're confident in your quality and service, that risk is minimized.

Of course, you can always give gift certificates, brochures, free consultations, free demos, free seminars, free tours and a wealth of free information on your website.

In addition to these, guerrillas are creative in dreaming up what they might give for free. Of course, many advertising specialties such as calendars and scratch pads, mouse pads and ballpoint pens are emblazoned with their names and theme lines, but guerrillas exercise extra creativity as well.

The highest form of that creativity is displayed when they give for free what they ordinarily sell. HotMail attracted more than ten million customers for its free email service. Now, that service is supported by advertising. By ending each free email from the sender with an offer for free email for the recipient, HotMail used word-of-mouse to the ultimate.

It's true that some bozos will sign up for your freebie and then you'll never hear from them again. But many customers will be so impressed by your quality and service, your caring and dedication, that they'll end up making the purchase you want them to make. Many will become lifelong customers, making you forget those free-loading bozos entirely.

The investment of your free product or service for a limited time must be <u>measured against your current marketing investment</u>. But if you're a guerrilla, your quality and service will prove more than anything you can ever say in a marketing context. Your customers truly enjoy being your customers. Now, they know why you are so confident in your offering. <u>Nothing can substitute for an actual ownership experience.</u>

I realize that all companies cannot give what they sell for free, not even for a limited time. But if you can see daylight in giving your offering for free, you might lift your marketing to the highest level while forming bonds that might otherwise have never been established.

GUERRILLA EXERCISE:

1. List the things you currently give away at no cost.

2. List the other things you can, but currently do not give away.

3. List the businesses you patronize — listing only those which gave you something for free.

GUERRILLA ACTION STEPS:

1. List the free information supplied on your website. For example, there is a list of 100 guerrilla marketing weapons on my own website at JayConradLevinson.com. Promoting that free list attracts visitors to my site.

2. List the kind of information your customers and prospects would most appreciate, and then try to supply it at no cost on your website — or even in printed form.

3. Put a check next to the items you currently offer for free:

    _____ Newsletter

    _____ Consultations

    _____ Demonstrations

    _____ Samples

_____ Trial Offers

_____ Seminars and Clinics

_____ Talks at Clubs and Associations

CHAPTER 12

Getting Extra Mileage From Your Marketing And From Email

GETTING EXTRA MILEAGE FROM YOUR MARKETING AND FROM EMAIL

Don't limit your marketing merely to the media you're using. Market it all over the place. Anything worth promoting is worth cross-promoting. During the trying days of a rugged economy, this is a crucial strategy.

Guerrillas know that all the media work better if they're supported by the other media. Put your web site onto your TV commercial. Mention your advertising in your direct mail. Refer to your direct mail in your telemarketing. Plant the seeds of your offering with some kinds of marketing and fertilize them with other kinds.

You're not really promoting unless you're cross-promoting. Your trade show booth will be far more valuable to you if you promote it in trade magazines and with fliers put under the doors of hotels near the trade show. Guerrillas try to market their marketing.

Your prospects, being humans, are eclectic people. They pay attention to a lot of media so you can't depend on a mere one medium to motivate a purchase. You're got to introduce a notion, remind people of it, say it again, and then repeat it in different words somewhere else. That share of mind for which guerrilla strive? They get it when they combine several media. They say in their ads, "Call or write for our free brochure."

They say in their Yellow Pages ad, "Get even more details at our website." They enclose a copy of their magazine ad in their mailing. They blow up a copy to use as a sign. Their website features their print ads.

Guerrillas are quick to mention their use of one medium while using another because they realize that people equate broad scale marketing with quality and success. They know that people trust names they've heard of much more than strange and new names, and guerrillas are realistic enough to know that people miss most marketing messages — often intentionally. The remote control is not only a way to save their steps but also a method of eliminating marketing messages.

No matter how glorious their newspaper campaign may be, guerrillas realize that not all of their prospects read the paper so they've got to get to these people in another way. No matter how dazzling their website, it's like a grain of sand in a desert if it is not pointed out to an unknowing and basically uncaring public.

Cross-promoting in the media is another way to accomplish the all-important task of repetition. One way to repeat yourself and implant your message is to say it over and over again. Another way is to say it in several different places. Guerrillas try to do both. Nothing is left to chance. If you saw a yellow pages ad that made you an offer from a company you've never heard of and another with the same offer except that the ad said, "As advertised on television," you'd probably opt for the second because of that added smidgen of credibility. I rest my case.

The psychology of marketing requires basic knowledge of human behavior. Human beings do not like making decisions in a hurry and are not quick to develop relationships. They certainly do want relationships, but they've been stung in the past and they don't want to be stung again.

They have learned well to distrust much marketing because of its proclivity to exaggeration. All too many times they've read of sales at stores and learned that only a tiny selection of items were on sale. They've been bamboozled more times than you'd think by the notorious fine print on contracts. And they've been high pressured by more than one salesperson.

That's why they process your marketing communications in their unconscious minds, eventually arriving at their decisions because of an emotional reason even though they may say they are deciding based on logic. They factor a lot about you into their final decision — how long they've heard of you, where your marketing appears, how it looks and feels to them, the quality of your offer, your convenience or lack of it, what others have said about you, and most of all, how your offering can be of benefit to their lives.

Although they state that they now want what you're selling, and they do it in a very conscious manner, you can be sure they were guided by their unconscious minds. The consistent communicating of your benefits, your message and your name has penetrated their sacred unconscious mind. They've come to feel that they can trust you and so they decide to buy.

Any pothole in their road to purchasing at this point might dissuade them. They call to make an inquiry and they are treated shabbily on the phone? You've lost them. Do they access your website for more information and either find no website or find one littered with self-praise? You've lost them. They visit you and feel pressured or misunderstood? They're gone.

You've got to realize that the weakest point in your marketing can derail all the strong points. Excellence through and through, start to finish, is what people have come to expect from businesses, and these days, they won't settle for less. The insight you must have is that marketing is a 360 degree process and you've got to do it right from all angles at all times. When it comes to marketing, people have built-in alarm systems, and any shady behavior on your part sets the bells to clanging, the sirens screaming.

It is very difficult to woo a person from the brand they use right now to your brand. Although they are loathe to change, they do change. And when they do, they patronize businesses that understand the psychology of human beings and the true nature of marketing.

During tough times, guerrillas are very attuned to free methods of marketing. They are well aware that free marketing exists in its most free state as email, which is far more than merely letters with free postage.

Mark Twain said he never let his schooling interfere with his education. Regardless of your schooling, there's little chance it covered what technology makes possible today. If you took a course in how computers can aid your marketing, the first insight you would have gained would be into the profitability for you if you become savvy about email.

When you think of email, don't compare it with snail mail because it's considerably different. In fact, it is such an improvement on old-fashioned mail delivery that the U.S. Postal service now uses it, and today there is a lot more email being sent daily than snail mail. Soon, half of all bills and payments will be sent electronically. More than three-fourths of Social Security checks, tax refunds and other federal payments sent in 2004 went electronically.

In fact, the U.S. Postal Service is now in serious trouble because of the vast amount of information transmitted via the Internet. For much of this, guerrillas owe a tip of their propeller beanie to Ray Tomlinson who invented email in 1971.

You can use email in your marketing in ways that will make your customers delighted to be doing business with you. Guerrillas love email but hate junk email, known as spamming.

Their affinity to email is because they can deliver their messages instantly and to anywhere in the world if the recipients are online, as more and more of them are with each word I type. That means email saves you time in communicating and money that you used to spend on postage. It can also help save trees on the planet because it is so delightfully paperless.

Each recipient can read your email on screen or print and save it just as with a standard letter, which does use paper. But you don't have to print and save your email, saving you the cost of paper and the convenience of space. Save it in your computer. Make copies as you need them. All your files and memos can be kept in one convenient location. Each one is dated and timed. Many experts feel that for all the great things about being online, email is the most valuable of all computer applications.

Email also helps you save on the cost of courier service and faxing. Use it to send brief messages or long documents, to send black and white communications or colorful, beautifully-designed materials. It's easy for you and easy for the person who receives your email.

Who should that be? People who want to receive it, that's who. Find their names on your customer list, in the newsgroups to which you belong, in chat rooms where they're talking about your industry, possibly even your company. Although email isn't free, because you need a computer and an internet connection, it's far less expensive than telephoning, mailing or faxing. When using it, keep your message as brief as possible, because people read computer screens differently than letters. They know being online saves time, so they don't want to waste time reading long things. As Thomas Jefferson said, "Never use two words when one word will do."

You're aware, as all guerrillas are, of how such technology can strengthen your marketing. You must also be aware of its limitations and of the new advancements that are taking place at breakneck speed. Don't let those advancements overwhelm you. Very little becomes obsolete, but nearly everything becomes improved.

Technology, for all the wondrous things about it, can also be a major distraction and a drain on your time if you focus on the technology itself rather than on the benefits it can bring to your business.

As "Net Benefits" author Kim Elton reminds us, "Business is life and life is messy. Like a kitchen sink full of dirty dishes, you know that when you've finally cleaned them up, someone will burn a tuna casserole and you'll be back in sudsy water up to your elbows with a Brillo pad in no time. But if the kids are growing up healthy and strong — and helping out with the dishes now and then — it's worth all the effort. Soon you'll get a dishwasher and you can shift the mess from the sink to the dishwasher. The dishes still have to be cleaned. The technology eases the labor and takes away some of the pain, but it doesn't relieve the duty."

That's the insight that I want you to take from this lesson and from this course. Technology helps with the job but doesn't do the job. That's your task. In order for you to understand how technology can help you, it's not necessary for you to learn the technical jargon, the nerdy part of technology. But you must comprehend the impact of technology and the ways it can transform a squirt gun into a cannon.

To cash in on the transformation, you must be in close touch with your needs. Technology will help you meet them. You must know how best to utilize the technology in which you've invested to get the maximum benefit for the money you've put forth. You've got to recognize hype for just what it is and solid science for just what it is.

You wouldn't dream of running a business without using a telephone. The computer will be just as endemic as phones. Using technology will be as easy as making a phone call. Investment research company Robertson Stephens stated it this way:

"Communicating is becoming the primary role of computers after four decades of number crunching. We stand at a technology crossroads and are witnessing a technological metamorphosis... computers, originally designed for number crunching and applied to computing tasks for nearly 50 years, will be used in the future primarily for communicating." The future is now the present.

Now, you know how to market during tough times...and that's the best way to describe the present these days.

GUERRILLA EXERCISE:

1. List the ways you currently market your marketing.

2. Dig deep into your mind and list three other ways you can market your marketing.

3. Prepare a plan for using email during the next year. Putting it into writing helps it transform into a reality.

GUERRILLA ACTION STEPS:

1. Begin compiling a list of people to whom you'll send email. Get that list from your customer list, from people who will trade lists with you, from people who have registered for something from your website, and from your fusion marketing partners. Nobody appreciates spam, but almost everyone appreciates email targeted at their interests.

2. Make a list, based upon this course, of the marketing tactics you will begin to employ to make waves during tough times. Times may be tough for others — but tough times are golden opportunities for guerrillas.

NOTES:

NOTES:

GET THE COMPLETE GUERRILLA ARSENAL!

Guerrilla Marketing for the New Millennium

A complete reworking of Jay Conrad Levinson's guerrilla "manifesto". Learn to think and market like a guerrilla and crush your competitors.

ISBN: 1-933596-07-4   Paperback
ISBN: 1-933596-08-2   eBook
ISBN: 1-933596-09-0   CD Audio

Guerrilla Marketing: Put Your Advertising on Steroids

Jay Conrad Levinson takes the proven concepts of the world's most successful companies, and synthesized them into a new type of marketing that any business can use to make mega-profits. This is Barely Legal... But You Can Still Get Away With It!

ISBN: 1-933596-13-9   Paperback
ISBN: 1-933596-14-7   eBook
ISBN: 1-933596-15-5   CD Audio

Guerrilla Copywriting

60 Profitable Tips in 60 Enlightening Minutes. Jay Conrad Levinson and David Garfinkel join forces to give small business owners, executives and marketing professionals 60 essential tactics, strategies and concepts for producing highly effective marketing messages.

ISBN: 1-933596-20-1   CD Audio

Guerrilla Marketing During Tough Times

Find Out Why Your Business Is Slowing Down. Jay Conrad Levinson shows you exactly why your business is slowing down in tough economic times and exactly what you can do about it.

ISBN: 1-933596-10-4   Paperback
ISBN: 1-933596-11-2   eBook
ISBN: 1-933596-12-0   CD Audio

Guerrilla Marketing 101: Lessons From The Father Of Guerrilla Marketing — DVD/Workbook Bundle

This 4-Volume set contains over 5 hours of business-building secrets personally presented by Jay Conrad Levinson, Father of the Worldwide Guerrilla Marketing Revolution.

ISBN: 1-933596-16-3   Bundle
ISBN: 1-933596-17-1   DVD
ISBN: 1-933596-18-X   Workbook

Guerrilla Marketing 101: Lessons From The Father Of Guerrilla Marketing — Bootlegged

Over 4 hours of Bootlegged, CD Quality Audio, from the GM 101 Set. Never before revealed tactics and insights from the Father of Guerrilla Marketing.

ISBN: 1-933596-30-9   CD Audio

These items are available through bookstores or directly through Morgan James Publishing at http://www.MorganJamesPublishing.com.

136

GET YOUR FREE GIFT!

U ntil now, no marketing association in existence could make a business bulletproof. But once again, Jay Conrad Levinson, the most respected marketer in the world, has broken new ground. The Guerrilla Marketing Association is quite literally a blueprint for business immortality.

Receive a **two-month FREE trial membership** in the Guerrilla Marketing Association where Guerrilla Marketing coaches and leading business experts answer your business questions online and during exclusive weekly telephone chats. This $99 value is your gift for investing in *Guerrilla Marketing During Tough Times*.

Join right now before your competition does at http://www.Morgan-James.com/gma.

To purchase additional Guerrilla Marketing products by Jay Conrad Levinson, visit the Morgan James Publishing Bookstore at http://www.MorganJamesPublishing.com.

www.ingramcontent.com/pod-product-compliance
Lightning Source LLC
Jackson TN
JSHW020021141224
75386JS00025B/635